HOW TO DEVELOP ASSERTIVENESS

Sam R Lloyd

First published in the United States of America in 1988 by Crisp Publications Inc, 95 First Street, Los Altos, California 94022, USA

This edition first published in Great Britain in 1988 by Kogan Page Ltd, 120 Pentonville Road, London N1 9JN

Reprinted 1989, 1990, 1991, 1993, 1994

British Library Cataloguing in Publication Data

Lloyd, Sam R.
How to develop assertiveness: practical techniques for personal success – (Better management skills)
1. Self-assertion
I. Title II. Series
158′.1

ISBN 1–85091–809–0
ISBN 1–85091–810–4 Pbk

Typeset by the Castlefield Press, Wellingborough
Printed and bound in Great Britain by
Biddles Ltd, Guildford and King's Lynn

Contents

About This Book 5

Preface 6

Introduction 7

An Assertiveness Quiz 9

1. How to Develop Assertiveness 13
Which is which? – a quick quiz *14*
Can you really get there from here? *15*
A personality quiz *16*
A people-watching case history *18*

2. Ensuring Successful Change 21
The five Ps of successful change *21*
Are you using the right maps? *23*
Self-fulfilling prophecy *24*
An assertive philosophy *26*
More about self-fulfilling prophecy *27*
Programming yourself for success *28*
Your reprogramming statements *31*

3. Feelings: The Emotional Component of Assertiveness 33
Choice and win-win relationships *36*
Talking about feelings *37*
Developing emotional awareness *38*

4. Changing Your Behaviour 39
Choose assertive words carefully *39*
Some dos and don'ts *42*
Body language *43*
Stop signs *49*
Green lights *50*

5. Expanding Your Assertiveness 51
Four assertive styles *51*
Which style is which? – a quiz *52*
Sending assertive messages *55*
Can you identify these people? *57*
How delivery affects different styles *58*
Stay on the right road–goal setting *59*
Give yourself credit for success *60*

6. Summary and Review 63

About This Book

How to Develop Assertiveness stands out from other self-help books in an important way. It's not a book to read, it's a book to *use*. The unique 'self-paced' format of this book encourages a reader to get involved and try some new ideas immediately.

This book will provide an awareness and understanding of what assertive behaviour is and why it is desirable and important for you to develop and use assertive behaviour in your natural style. Using the simple yet sound techniques presented can help any reader learn to become more assertive.

How to Develop Assertiveness can be used effectively in a number of ways. Here are some possibilities:

- *Self-study*. Because the book is self-instructional, all that is needed is a quiet place, and some time. By completing the activities and exercises, a reader should receive valuable ideas about how to become more assertive.
- *Workshops and seminars*. The book is ideal for assigned reading prior to a workshop or seminar. With the basics in hand, the quality of the participation will improve, and more time can be spent on concept extensions and applications during the programme. The book is also effective when it is distributed at the beginning of a session, and participants work through the contents.
- *Open learning*. Books can also be sent to those unable to attend 'home office' training sessions.

There are several other possibilities that depend on the objectives, programme or ideas of the user.

Preface

This book is for anyone who wants to take charge and live life. Developing assertiveness can be influential in creating personal success and making things happen for you.

Will reading this book result in your being assertive? Not if all you do is read. If, however, you read and complete the exercises and practise the techniques as recommended, you will learn how to develop assertiveness. The book can't make you assertive, but you can!

Developing assertiveness is more than just learning to talk differently. Being assertive requires *thinking* assertively, *feeling* confident, and *behaving* positively. In this book you will learn how to develop each of these aspects of assertiveness. Explanations of personality and psychological concepts will help you to understand yourself and other people. Guidelines for word choices and behaviour will help you to change how you interact with others. Several exercises will help you to change attitudes that interfere with your being assertive.

Assertive people enjoy their work, play, friends and family. Assertive people are effective, vital, and valued by others. With this book, some personal commitment and a little time, you can become an assertive person and experience these benefits for the rest of your life!

Sam R. Lloyd

Introduction

Assertive behaviour and why it is important

What do you think of when you hear the word 'assertive'? Many people think of someone adamantly standing their ground, pushing for his or her own way, refusing to give an inch. Others think of someone who is generally pleasant but stubborn on certain issues. Most people don't understand what assertive behaviour really is.

Assertive behaviour, as defined in this book, is a natural style that is nothing more than being direct, honest, and respectful while interacting with others. So why is there a need for assertiveness training courses and books? Why do people poke fun at assertiveness training? Why does management in some organisations resist when assertive training is mentioned?

The poking fun and open resistance are symptoms of a lack of understanding. When people do not understand it is normal to resist change. We believe that assertiveness is the most desirable human behaviour! It is needed for honest, healthy relationships. It is the behaviour required for 'win-win' outcomes in negotiation (when both parties feel a sense of achievement), conflict resolution, family life, and normal business dealings.

As more people develop assertiveness and influence others, the awareness and acceptance of assertiveness will increase. This book explains why people have to make a conscious effort to develop their assertiveness. Even though assertive behaviour *is* natural it is not the only natural behaviour! We humans also use non-assertive and aggressive behaviour. These styles create many problems in our relationships, business dealings and social interactions.

All of us use all three behaviour styles throughout our lives. Most of us are not as consistently assertive as we might think. When we learn to become more assertive we can reduce our conflicts, failures, dissatisfactions, and stresses. Developing assertiveness requires effort, but the rewards are worth it. This book will provide you with information, simple directions and plenty of opportunities to practise becoming more assertive.

After first finding out how assertive you are right now, you will then learn how to identify the three behaviour styles previously mentioned (assertive, non-assertive and aggressive) and how to ensure successful change and develop assertiveness. Once you have learned to develop your assertiveness, you will finally learn how to maintain the changes you have made. All of this in less than 70 pages.

The first step is to find out how assertive you are now.

An Assertiveness Quiz

Before learning how to develop assertiveness, it is important to take a few moments to get some idea of where you are now. Answer the questions below honestly. They will help you to gain some insights about your current level of assertiveness.

Assign a number to each item using this scale:

Always				Never
5	4	3	2	1

______ 1. I ask others to do things without feeling guilty or anxious.

______ 2. When someone asks me to do something I don't want to do, I say 'No' without feeling guilty or anxious.

______ 3. I am comfortable when speaking to a large group of people.

______ 4. I confidently express my honest opinions to authority figures (such as my boss).

______ 5. When I experience powerful feelings (anger, frustration, disappointment, etc), I express them easily.

______ 6. When I express anger, I do so without blaming others for 'making me cross'.

______ 7. I am comfortable speaking out in a group.

______ 8. If I disagree with the majority opinion in a meeting, I can 'stick to my guns' without feeling uncomfortable or being abrasive.

______ 9. When I make a mistake, I will acknowledge it.

______ 10. I tell others when their behaviour creates a problem for me.

______ 11. Meeting new people socially is something I do with ease and comfort.

______ 12. When discussing my beliefs, I do so without labelling the opinions of others as 'crackpot', 'stupid', 'ridiculous', 'irrational'.

______ 13. I assume that most people are competent and trustworthy and do not have difficulty delegating tasks to others.

______ 14. When considering undertaking something I have never done before, I feel confident I can learn to do it.

______ 15. I believe my needs are as important as those of others and I am entitled to have my needs satisfied.

TOTAL SCORE

How assertive are you?

If your total is 60 or higher, you have a consistently assertive philosophy and probably handle most situations well. You may receive some ideas from this book to improve your skills and effectiveness still more.

If your total is 45–60, you have a fairly assertive outlook. There are some situations in which you may be naturally assertive, but the book will help you to increase your assertiveness through practice.

If your total is 30–45, you seem to be assertive in some situations but your natural response is either unassertive or aggressive. Using the suggestions in this book to change some perceptions and practising new behaviour should allow you to handle things much more assertively in the future.

If your total is 15–30, you have considerable difficulty being assertive. If you follow the road outlined in this book, practise, and allow yourself time to grow and change; you can become much more comfortable in situations where asserting yourself is important.

CHAPTER 1

How to Develop Assertiveness

It would be nice if you could simply decide to go down the road marked 'Assertive' and live your life without straying from the path.

Real life is full of twists and turns and *no one is consistently assertive*. All of us use the three basic behaviour styles described below, depending on the situation and personal factors. The good news is that *we can learn to become more assertive more of the time*.

1. *Non-assertive* behaviour is passive and indirect. It communicates a message of inferiority. By being non-assertive we allow the wants, needs, and rights of others to be more important than our own. Non-assertive behaviour helps to create 'win-lose' situations. A person behaving non-assertively will lose while allowing others to win (or at best be disregarded). Following this road leads to being a victim, not a winner.
2. *Aggressive* behaviour is more complex. It can be either active or passive. Aggression can be direct or indirect, honest or dishonest – but it always communicates an impression of superiority and disrespect. By being aggressive we put our wants, needs, and rights above those of others. We attempt to get our way by not allowing others a choice. Aggressive behaviour is usually inappropriate because it violates the rights of others. People behaving aggressively may 'win' by making sure others 'lose' – but in doing so set themselves up for retaliation. No one likes a bully.
3. *Assertive* behaviour is active, direct, and honest. It communicates an impression of self-respect and respect for

others. By being assertive we view our wants, needs, and rights as equal with those of others. We work towards 'win-win' outcomes. An assertive person wins by influencing, listening, and negotiating, so that others choose to cooperate willingly. This behaviour leads to success without retaliation and encourages honest, open relationships!

Which is which? – a quick quiz

Identify each behaviour style in the following examples and write your answer in the space.

Use the abbreviations: NAS = Non-assertive, AS = Assertive, AG = Aggressive, then check your answers with those of the author.

______ 1. 'Only an idiot would think of a solution like that! Don't you ever think before you talk?'

______ 2. 'You know, we might want to think about a different alternative. What do you think?'

______ 3. 'Oh, I can't go – I have other plans.'

______ 4. 'I'm not completely comfortable with your solution. Will you please develop at least one more option?'

______ 5. 'No, thank you. I appreciate your asking, but I really don't enjoy opera.'

______ 6. 'Opera! You've got to be kidding!'

______ 7. 'This probably isn't what you wanted, but I wasn't too sure about what you said, and, anyway, I'm not very good at this kind of thing.'

______ 8. 'Well, all right, if that's what you want to do.'

______ 9. 'Good idea! Let's do it!'

______ 10. 'Tracy, please send this to all regional offices today.'

Ready to check your answers? The author's are below with brief explanatory comments.

Answers

1. AG–Accusatory, exaggerated, blameful, invites defensiveness.
2. NAS–Hesitant, passive, apologetic, invites disregard.
3. NAS–Plans are only plans and can be changed. This is subtle dishonesty and is one of the most common ways of avoiding having to say 'No'.
4. AS–Honest, respectful, invites cooperation.
5. AS–Honest, tactful, firm but appreciative (compare with 3).
6. AG–Sarcastic, blameful, invites defensiveness.
7. NAS–Self-depreciating, defensive, invites disrespect.
8. NAS–Hesitant, deferential, possibly dishonest about wants.
9. AS–Enthusiastic, genuine, cooperative.
10. AS–Direct, respectful, invites cooperation.

Later in this book some guidelines, activities and examples of word choices and accompanying body language will be presented. These guidelines will help you to learn how to communicate assertively. Understanding and recognising different communication styles bring an important awareness upon which to build new skills.

Can you really get there from here?

Do you believe you can't change your basic personality? If so, you and the experts agree. Most experts concur that a general 'personality type' cannot be changed. Once you have developed your basic personality (between the ages of five and twelve), your most natural psychological characteristics do not really change much.

If this is the case, you might ask, 'Is it a waste of time to engage in self-improvement?' The answer is No! Even if your core characteristics are permanent, it is possible to change many things about yourself. Things you can change include your beliefs, attitudes, goals, expectations, word choices, and body language, to mention a few. *Modestly changing any of these factors can result in your being assertive more often. When this happens, you win!*

Before we work out in which direction you need to travel, it will be helpful if you understand your starting point. Answer the items below (as honestly as you can) to gain a better awareness of your personality characteristics. (Your spontaneous, natural response will provide the most accurate insights.)

A personality quiz

True or False

______ 1. I almost always speak or make eye contact first when encountering another person.

______ 2. I prefer being with several people rather than having a one-to-one social conversation.

______ 3. I prefer to eat lunch alone.

______ 4. The best way to make a decision is to assemble all the facts first.

______ 5. When I want to have fun, I do something exciting, something with lots of action.

______ 6. The most important thing in life is having good relationships with family and friends.

______ 7. When I go to meetings or parties, I spend most of the time talking with one person at a time rather than interacting with a group.

______ 8. The best way to learn something is to jump in and do it.

_______ 9. I am very aware of how others respond to me and often worry about whether they like me or if I have displeased them.

_______ 10. When I make a decision I trust my intuition – somehow I seem to sense what is best.

_______ 11. I am usually the one to initiate things, either social activities or business.

_______ 12. Spending an evening discussing current events, work-related topics, or philosophical issues can be very stimulating and interesting.

_______ 13. When I am with others we usually discuss relationships, personal difficulties, or how we feel about our lives.

_______ 14. My favourite topic is what people have done, where they have been, and what happened. I enjoy telling others about my adventures.

Answers

If you answered 1, 4, 7, 11 and 12 TRUE and the others FALSE, you are an active initiator who prefers one-to-one interaction. You seem to be a THINKER who plans and you are careful and methodical.

If you answered 2, 6, 9, 10, 11 and 13 TRUE and most others FALSE, you seem to be an active initiator who is social and caring. You are a FEELER in touch with your emotions. You value personal relationships and want to please people.

If you answered 5, 8, 10 and 14 TRUE and most others FALSE, you are more passive than initiative with people. You are less involved with people and more interested in physical activities. You are a DOER who enjoys the pleasure of being active. You are not likely to be comfortable around others when they discuss feelings.

What about question 3? If you like to eat lunch alone, this indicates that you need solitude. THINKERS and some DOERS are often more withdrawing than involving. This means they are comfortable being alone. Most FEELERS, many THINKERS, and some DOERS have a greater need to be with people.

There are many other psychological groupings. There are also more sophisticated questionnaires which identify these groups. In this book, we have tried to keep things simple and have limited ourselves to three general groupings; THINKERS, FEELERS, and DOERS. These three are sufficient to provide insight into some of the most basic *automatic* behaviour styles and orientations towards life. Awareness of which group you are in should help you to understand why you are more comfortable in certain situations than others. It also helps to explain why others often approach life differently from you.

Each personality type is all right. It is natural to consider the group we identify with as somehow better than the others. One type, however, is no better than another, it is simply different. All types are essential and all contribute to life, organisations, and families. Each has different strengths and each approaches work and life differently. *Accepting this reality is an important step to develop an* assertive *win-win approach with others*.

A people-watching case history

At a professional conference the following people were observed at the social gathering held at the conclusion of the first day. John arrived exactly on time, paused at the entrance of the room to survey the crowd and purposefully walked to the refreshment area to obtain a drink. After getting his drink, he looked around again and saw someone he knew. Approaching his acquaintance, he made eye contact and spoke, 'Hello, Mary. Have you been here long?' They talked for some time and the man returned to the refreshment area while looking around the room again. Which type is John?

Martha arrived after John. She entered the room and immediately walked towards a group of four people who were near. She introduced herself, 'Hello, I'm Martha and I'm really enjoying the conference. Are you?' She quickly met everyone and joined in their conversation about the day. Soon the group was sharing information about their families. Martha noticed a friend arrive, waved with a big smile, and motioned her friend to come and join the group. Which type is Martha?

Sometime later Paula arrived. She had been returning some telephone calls and completing an analysis of a colleague's proposal, as she had promised she would. When Paula arrived she paused at the door to see if she recognised anyone. Seeing someone she knew, Paula walked over and the pair spent the entire time in an involved conversation about the problems of world peace. Which type is Paula?

Right after Paula entered the room, Bob arrived. He burst into the room, rushed to the refreshment area for a drink, spotted some people he had seen earlier and walked over to them. Someone looked up at him and Bob said, 'Hey! Where's the party? Nothing's happening – let's get something going here!' Within a few minutes the group left the social to go to part of the town where Bob had learned that live entertainment was available.

After finding the area, the group went to a building which housed several night clubs that offered dancing. Bob turned out to be an expert dancer and spent the evening dancing with various members of the group. Which type is Bob?

Answers

Easy, isn't it? John was a THINKER, Martha was a FEELER, Paula was another THINKER, and Bob was a DOER. All four are successful individuals and lead happy, meaningful lives. They all have different styles and react differently to situations.

To one degree or another, all personality types use all three behaviour styles. With better awareness and practice, it is possible to increase assertiveness and decrease non-assertive and aggressive choices. Simply stated, all of us can learn to change.

CHAPTER 2
Ensuring Successful Change

Any change, large or small, is challenging. Many psychotherapists are aware that for many people significant change usually occurs only after some traumatic experience. You don't have to wait for some traumatic event to trigger change, but you do need to be prepared for change, to make certain that change will be successful. The following guidelines will help to guarantee any successful changes you wish to make.

The five Ps of successful change

1. Protection

Change is often scary! Have you ever made a New Year's resolution and failed to keep it? One reason we don't change, even when we truly want to, is fear. Often our fear is vague and unidentified, but it is enough to sabotage changing. Protection can help you stick with a commitment to change. Here are some protection suggestions:

- Start your change in your safest environment.
- Change one thing at a time – slow and easy does it.
- Whenever you feel unsure or anxious, answer these questions:
  'What's the worst that can happen?'
  'What's the probability that it will happen?'
  'What can I do to prevent it or reduce the probability?'

2. Potency

Change is an active process, not a passive one. To activate your personal power it is necessary to invest some mental effort, emotional involvement, and physical activity to changing. You can learn to tap into your potency if you:

- Define your change goal in simple, active, positive words.
- Write your change goal and display it where you see it daily.
- Imagine yourself practising your change goal and visualise yourself doing it well.
- Tell yourself daily, 'I can . . . ', 'I will . . . ', and 'I am . . .'.

3. Permission

Each of us requires permission to change. Be sure to give yourself permission and also get permission from others, significant in your life, who will be affected by your changes. Without their permission and support, you may not succeed.

- Tell each person what you plan to do and why.
- Ask each, 'Is that all right with you?'

Most significant others will appreciate your consideration of their involvement with your changes. Most will say 'go for it' when you ask. If someone says 'No', identify the reason for their reluctance. It might be an important issue to explore and could help you redefine your goal.

You do not need permission from everyone who is important in your life to change, but having permission from them will ease the pressure on you and normally result in having a better support system. Successful people know how important it is to accept the help and support of others!

4. Practice

Whether learning to ride a bicycle, program a computer, play a musical instrument, or use assertive behaviour, intellectual comprehension of concepts is not all it takes. (Sorry, all you THINKERS.) To become skilful in any behaviour requires *practice.* A great deal of practice may be needed before a new behaviour style becomes natural and integrated.

- Decide what to practise and how it can best be accomplished.
- Develop a practice schedule. Be specific about how often,

when, and where. Record your efforts.
- Allow yourself to make mistakes. Remember, it is practice and you don't have to be perfect!

5. Proof

When your practice goes well and you experience satisfaction, you are receiving *proof* that you can change. This provides valuable *reinforcement* which encourages you to do it again. New behaviour must be reinforced repeatedly with positive experiences (proof) to keep the process working and ensure a permanent change.

- Ask others to give you positive feedback about your practice.
- Give yourself 'pats on the back' with positive self-talk.
- Establish a practice schedule and reward yourself for keeping your commitment. Give yourself a reward just for practising. You don't have to be completely changed to deserve some positive reinforcement.

Are you using the right maps?

In the preface of this book you read that developing assertiveness requires THINKING assertively, FEELING confident, and BEHAVING positively. In this section you will learn some ways to change your thinking – attitudes, expectations, beliefs, and perceptions. As long as your thinking is non-assertive or aggressive, you will continue to choose those behaviour styles. Becoming assertive may require you to change how you think about yourself, other people, and life in general.

Practising new behaviour styles is an important part of developing your assertiveness. Later you will receive specific suggestions which will help you. Before you begin to practise, however, another important factor requires your attention. Your expectations about learning to be more assertive will have a strong influence on your success.

How realistic are your expectations?

Complete the following assessment to gain some insight into your expectations, then check your responses with those of the author.

Agree or disagree (A or D)

______ 1. If people know too much about you they can use this information against you.
______ 2. If everything is going smoothly, look out! Something is bound to go wrong soon.
______ 3. There is a potential positive outcome to any problem or adverse situation.
______ 4. If you want something done properly, you must do it yourself.
______ 5. Bad luck comes in threes.
______ 6. When you smile, the world smiles with you.
______ 7. Everyone deserves recognition – not just those who excel.
______ 8. The rich get richer and the poor get poorer.
______ 9. It's all right to admit mistakes – people respect honesty.
______ 10. New people, new situations and new experiences are fun and exciting.

Self-fulfilling prophecy

Have you ever heard of self-fulfilling prophecy? This phenomenon often happens without our conscious awareness of it. Self-fufilling prophecy is the phenomenon that results in our experiencing what we expect to experience. It is our getting from others just what we thought we would. We often succeed or fail because we subconsciously 'knew' we would!

Our lives are full of examples of this. Have you ever thought, 'I'll never get this finished on time!' and then proved yourself

If you agreed with 1, 2, 4 and 5 you are reflecting consistently negative expectations, particularly about people. If you agreed with 3, 6, 9, and 10 you have a positive outlook. If you agreed with 7 you appear to be generous and realistic. If you agreed with 2 and 8 you seem to feel you have little control over life.

right? Have you noticed that some people approach situations with an 'I can't do this' attitude and experience problems and failures, while others approach the same situations with an 'I can' attitude and succeed? Expectations and attitudes are powerful influences on actual outcomes.

A case history

A brilliant young woman named Joyce was leaving home to attend college, but was concerned about her ailing mother. Her mother reassured Joyce and told her to go and be successful in her college studies. She said, 'Don't worry dear. I'll live to see you graduate!'

Joyce went to college and performed at a superior level. During the first term of her second year she began to experience insomnia, loss of appetite, and struggled with her studies. Her marks fell but she passed her exams. Her last term was a disaster! Joyce's health continued to deteriorate and she dropped her most difficult classes. This involved longer attendance before she would graduate.

At the beginning of the next term, Joyce's friends were concerned about her continued weight loss and general poor health. They encouraged her to seek help. Her doctor could find no explanation for her condition and arranged for her to see a psychologist. The psychologist uncovered Joyce's deep concern for her mother. The psychologist heard Joyce repeat her mother's pledge, 'I'll live to see you graduate!' Her subconscious had interpreted that message as 'I will die once you graduate'. This simple phrase triggered an unconscious mechanism to delay graduation in order to keep mother alive.

After counselling, Joyce was able to complete her studies and graduate with honours.

Do you believe in self-fulfilling prophecy? If not, you should, because it is a well-documented phenomenon. Controlled research has shown that teachers, trainers, managers, parents, etc influence (often unintentionally) the behaviour of their students, employees, and/or children. Every day, subtle messages are delivered which communicate strong expectations.

Expectations, beliefs, attitudes, and values are communicated constantly through our words, facial expressions, posture, eye contact, voice tones, and behaviour. Without intending to, we influence others and reinforce in them what we expect from them. Thus, we get just what we thought we would.

If you expect employees to complain, they will. If you expect them to be trustworthy and hard-working, they will be. It is what you *truly expect*, not what you say you want; it is not what you purport to believe in, but what you *really believe* that counts. Some managers say they have an 'open door' but everyone knows their true message is 'don't bother me'. Parents may say, 'We love you because you're you and a B grade is fine'. However, if mum and dad really want all As, their message will be communicated regardless of what they *say*.

How does this relate to being assertive? Assertive behaviour comes more naturally when your core belief is that of an assertive philosophy. Whenever your expectations are non-assertive or aggressive, it is easy to send a double message when you wish to be assertive. Is there anything you can do? We think so. For openers you should read the following 'Assertive philosophy' often. Read it with conviction. Say the words aloud as though you sincerely believe them. If you genuinely wish to adopt a more assertive belief system, your perspective will begin to change and you will become more aware of the truth of the statements in your daily experience.

An assertive philosophy

1. I recognise that everyone has well practised communication habits and long standing attitudes that support and defend these habits.
2. I accept the communication habits of others as fact.

3. I will offer assertive communication and a 'win-win' attitude even when others are offering non-assertive or aggressive styles.
4. I understand that people change only when they choose to change.
5. I select my personal standard of communication rather than react to those of others.
6. I know others are different from me and all kinds of people are all right.
7. I accept responsibility for my feelings, thoughts, opinions, and behaviour. I realise I cannot be responsible for the feelings, thoughts, opinions, and behaviour of others.
8. I accept that every relationship involves each person having 50 per cent of the responsibility for the success or failure of that relationship.
9. I know that being non-assertive and aggressive is part of being human.
10. I know that every assertive choice precludes a non-assertive or aggressive choice and improves the chances for success at work and at home.

More about self-fulfilling prophecy

Self-fulfilling prophecy has a flip side. When you deliver a speech knowing people will be interested and amused, sure enough, that's the way you experience it. But, if you are anxious about the crowd being bored and unresponsive, you will probably have a miserable experience.

People who expect things to go wrong, (ie, who expect 'foreigners' to be inhospitable, who expect to have no fun, who dread meeting strangers etc), invariably have just such experiences again and again. *To create positive outcomes you must start with positive expectations!*

In the next section, you will learn about words and behaviour to practise to become more assertive. When you start practising the new ways of expressing yourself and handling situations, it is a good idea also to practise the technique of 'positive mental imagery'.

Positive mental imagery is nothing more than using your

imagination to visualise yourself saying and doing things successfully and assertively. Imagine situations where you *see* yourself *being* assertive. *Feel* confident, powerful and effective. *Hear* your voice sound strong and steady. *Experience* the satisfaction and pleasure of *being* assertive.

Do this repeatedly. Do it before you give a business presentation, before you ask an important question, before you introduce yourself to a stranger etc. The more powerful your mental image and expectation, the greater the success you should experience.

Remember – only imagine positive outcomes. Don't think about the possibilities of things going badly because your subconscious expectations are so powerful that failure could undermine your confidence and ultimate success. Recall the earlier situation of the student whose subconscious mind kept her from graduating because of a single powerful image planted years earlier.

Use the power of self-fulfilling prophecy to create positive experiences. When you are able to do this you have begun to develop an assertive philosophy. Think of positive mental imagery as programming a flight plan. Having the right expectations and perceptions before you start your journey is essential if you are to reach your planned destination safely.

Programming yourself for success

Positive mental imagery

Positive mental imagery is an exercise requiring conscious effort. It is a way to influence the subconscious mind. Subconscious expectations and internal dialogues are powerful influences on our perception of reality, our emotions and behaviour. Much of what exists in our subconscious was 'recorded' in early life and can be thought of as a 'psychological programme'.

Techniques to change both THINKING and FEELING patterns to help you become more assertive are explained in this section. You will learn to design a 'psychological programme' which will help to support your conscious efforts.

Reprogramming yourself

Much of the original 'psychological programming' has been with us from childhood and prompts our non-assertive, assertive and/or aggressive behaviour patterns. You cannot remove your original programming, but you can insert some new data to counteract that which is problematical.

Unlike a computer, a person cannot be totally reprogrammed. With a computer, it is possible to create a new program and run it immediately. The computer does not have to 'unlearn' old habits. With people, new programming must be done gradually and the new 'program' must be 'run' numerous times before things become automatic. But, it *can be done*!

How do you know what to put into your program? How do you enter the new data? Review the quiz items on pages 9–11 and 24. These will help you to recognise your beliefs, attitudes, perceptions, or expectations that are not consistent with an assertive philosophy. Listening carefully to what you say and do can provide additional 'shoulds' and 'should nots' that are inconsistent with your being assertive. Keep a journal in which you record your thoughts and internal dialogue. Study it and it will reveal a number of old 'programming messages' that you can change to improve your assertiveness.

To create a plan which will help you to reprogramme yourself, write out new statements which will counteract old behaviour. This plan should include *Permissions* (It's all right to . . . , I can . . .), *Commitments* (I will . . .) and *Affirmations* (I am . . .). These statements must be WRITTEN in SIMPLE, ACTIVE, and POSITIVE form. If they are complex, passive, or negative, you will not get good results.

Start with only a few (four or five) reprogramming statements. Write each statement on a 3 × 5 inch card. This card is handy to carry with you in a pocket, handbag, or briefcase. To use the reprogramming cards most effectively, you should be relaxed. To achieve deep relaxation you can sit in a hot tub or take a bubble bath, listen to soothing music, rest after exercising vigorously or meditate. Once relaxed, read each card aloud several times – hear the words, believe them, let them sink into your relaxed mind.

Inserting ideas into your conscious but highly relaxed mind will help you to open your *subconscious* to receive the input. 'Programmes' are stored in our subconscious mind and you must 'reprogramme' your subconscious before it can support your new objectives. Read your cards regularly for several weeks to condition your mind. You can read your cards any time for additional reinforcement, but using the 'reprogramming' routine before sleep is particularly powerful because your subconscious is active periodically during sleep (that's why we dream). Your subconscious will absorb what your conscious mind heard before sleep if you use the routine regularly.

To review, the simple steps to reprogramme yourself include:

1. Write simple, active, positive statements that you want to record (one per card).
2. Achieve a state of deep relaxation.
3. Read each statement aloud several times.
4. Sleep and let your subconscious absorb the ideas.
5. Do this daily for 21 days.

Sample statements

Following are some sample statements. You may wish to use these (or others you create) for your initial reprogramming.

Your statements should reflect your own objectives and needs. The most important statements are those which will help you to change old patterns of thinking and behaving. You are the person who is best equipped to identify what you want and need to change and to create a new programme to support this change.

Examples

It's all right for my wants and needs to be as important as those of others.
I can get my needs met.
I will ask for what I want.
I am someone who deserves to have my needs met.

It's all right to have feelings and express them.
I can express my feelings openly and honestly.

I will tell others what I am feeling.
I am an emotionally honest person.

It's all right to make mistakes or not know something.
I can admit my mistakes or say 'I don't know'.
I will admit my mistakes and say 'I don't know' when asked.
I am honest and will learn from my mistakes.
I can allow others to make mistakes.
I will have reasonable expectations of others.
I am realistic and understand that everyone makes mistakes.

It's all right to trust others.
I can share and trust.
I will trust and share.
I am a trusting and sharing person.

Your reprogramming statements

Now that you have the idea, write some SIMPLE, ACTIVE, POSITIVE statements for yourself. They can be in any of the following forms. The Affirmations (I am . . .) are probably the most powerful, but your *subconscious must believe* these statements for them to work. Using permissions and commitments as a starting point may help.

Your reprogramming statements

Permissions:
1. It's all right to
2. It's all right to
3. It's all right to

Permissions:
1. I can
2. I can
3. I can

Commitments:
1. I will
2. I will
3. I will

Affirmations:

1. I am
2. I am
3. I am

Remember, don't use too many statements – only four or five initially. You have plenty of time to expand your behaviour modification. Change is more effective a step at a time. This system *works* if you stay with it and give it an opportunity to work for you.

While reprogramming your subconscious each evening, you should also practise the new behaviour you desire on a daily basis. Chapter 4 will help you to learn how to do that.

CHAPTER 3

Feelings: The Emotional Component of Assertiveness

Human beings are emotional creatures! All of us have feelings of some sort every waking moment. The emotional component of developing our assertiveness can be one of our most challenging undertakings. One reason for this is that most of us learn about feelings which do not support assertiveness. A few of these lessons will be reviewed in this section and some new ideas will be put forth to help you to learn to use your emotions as you develop your assertiveness.

One lesson transmitted in most cultures goes something like this: 'Girls (women) are emotional; Boys (men) are unemotional and rational.' A true statement? Not really; everyone is emotional. Boys and men often don't learn about emotional honesty because they are taught early that they 'aren't supposed to be emotional'. Girls and women often learn exaggerated emotional responses to situations because they 'are supposed to be emotional'.

Another lesson is often labelled 'The Feeling Myth'. Most of us grow up believing that people can make each other feel. For example, do you believe that you can make someone angry? Do you worry about being assertive and 'hurting someone's feelings'? This myth teaches us to believe that our words and actions literally cause other people to feel the emotions they feel. It teaches us to believe that we have no choice about our own feelings. It also teaches us to believe that we are responsible for one another's feelings.

Why is it called myth? Because it is not true! FEELINGS ARE A CHOICE. Most people don't believe that statement when they first hear it or read it. You may not. Further explanation may help you to understand the truth of the statement.

One way to understand that feelings are a *choice* is to think about CAUSE and EFFECT. If words, actions or events make someone angry, frightened or sad, they have no choice. The person is *made* to feel that feeling. The word, action or event is the *cause* and the feeling is the *effect*. If the process truly were a cause and effect process, wouldn't it make sense that the same *cause* would then produce the same *effect* (feeling) in everyone? Simple observation proves that different people have different feelings about exactly the same event. Therefore it is the person receiving the words, actions or events who chooses an emotional response.

An example: If someone decided to surprise you for a birthday by hiring someone in a clown suit to show up at your work place and sing a song for you, how would you feel about the surprise? Whatever feeling you might have, you would probably agree that other people would respond differently to the same surprise. Some would be delighted and happy, others would feel embarrassed, others might get angry, and some might be disappointed. There is no sure way to predict anyone's emotional response in advance.

Granted, your emotional choice may be a strong habit. You might experience the same feeling in response to the same stimulus every time. This means you would perceive the process as being 'made to feel'. Realistically, you could choose a different emotional response even though it might feel unnatural at first.

Assertiveness demands emotional honesty. This is difficult to accomplish if you will not accept responsibility for your own feelings.

Another way to understand that we determine our feelings is to examine the process as an A B C system.

A = Stimulus (word, behaviour, event etc)
B = Internal dialogue or self-talk
C = Emotion

This whole process may happen in less than a second, but all three steps are always involved whenever we have an emotional response to something. Often it will seem that the feeling occurs simultaneously with the stimulus, but in a fraction of a second there was a sequence from A to C.

An example: While working in his office a man was interrupted by a special delivery. He looked at the envelope and noticed that it was from the city where his ex-wife lived. Immediately he felt anger and threw it on his desk saying, 'Why can't she just stay out of my life and let me live in peace?'

Did the envelope make him angry? Many people would answer yes. Obviously he wasn't angry before he received the special delivery and he got angry when he looked at it. Of course it made him angry.

What really happened was the A B C process. The man noticed the city of origin (A); assumed the letter came from his ex-wife and that it contained some unwanted intrusion on his life (B); and then felt angry (C). His anger was in response to his thoughts. He could just as easily have felt guilty, sad, anxious, or pleased.

To continue the story, the man read the message. As soon as he read it, he whooped loudly, started laughing, jumped up from his desk and did an impromptu dance around his office. Why the sudden change in emotion?

The message was from a client. The message was: 'Our board met today and considered your proposal. Thought you would like the news as soon as possible. We like your ideas and will double our business with you starting next month.' Upon reading this message (A); the man was thinking about a trip to the West Indies and how much praise he would receive from his boss (B); and became very happy (C). It was the same letter about which he first felt angry! The letter did not make him mad or glad. His self-talk influenced his choice of feelings.

Another important reason for understanding the truth about feelings is to learn to use more of your power. By allowing others to 'make you feel', you give the power to others. The old saying, 'Sticks and stones may break my bones, but names can never hurt me', has an element of truth. Knowing that when you feel hurt, embarrassed, angry, sad, or joyful, because of the words of others, you are *choosing* those feelings.

Choice and win-win relationships

Assertiveness is a win-win approach and philosophy. To build and maintain win-win relationships each person must accept responsibility for his or her own feelings, thoughts and behaviour. You cannot be solely responsible for the feelings of others because you do not 'make them feel'. You are responsible for what you say and do because your words and actions *invite* others to feel certain emotions. Whether they do or not is up to them!

Assertiveness requires us to accept responsibility for our thoughts, feelings, and behaviour and requires us to respect the thoughts, feelings, and behaviour of others. When an individual accepts these responsibilities and stops blaming others for his or her feelings, a giant step has been taken towards a win-win philosophy.

What feeling would you choose? Why?
In the following exercise read the situation (A) and write your spontaneous emotion in the space under (C). Once you identify your feeling, write in what your self-talk was under (B).

Situation (A)	*Self-talk* (B)	*Feeling* (C)
A driver changes lanes without warning and almost hits your car.	____________ ____________	____________
You are asked spontaneously by your boss to come forward at a company meeting and explain a project to 100 people.	____________ ____________	____________
You finish an important presentation for your boss and important clients. When you return to your seat a colleague tells you that your shirt tail/blouse is sticking through an open zipper.	____________ ____________	____________

Whatever feelings and self-talk you experienced for the situations on the preceding page are all right. There is nothing 'bad' about feeling angry, embarrassed or elated. Your responses might not be the most productive or logical for the situation, but feelings are not logical. To change how you respond to certain situations, begin by changing your internal dialogue.

To practise this idea of learning new emotional responses by changing self-talk, use the situations from the last exercise but create some different self-talk which will help you to have a positive feeling.

Situation	*Self-talk*	*Feeling*
Near accident	____________	____________
Speaking to 100 people	____________	____________
Open zip	____________	____________

Talking about feelings

An important part of developing assertiveness is expressing your honest emotions. Many people don't do that. Even if you understand that being emotional is and part of being human, you may need practice to talk about your feelings. The assertive way to express feelings is to say 'I feel . . . ', 'I felt . . . ', 'I'm feeling . . . ', 'I am . . . ', 'I was . . . ', 'I get . . . '. What follows each phrase is a word describing a feeling.

First you must know what you are feeling. To decide which emotion you are experiencing ask, 'What am I feeling – MAD, SAD, GLAD or SCARED?' Those are the four basic human emotions and this question is a good one to help you get in touch with your feelings quickly and accurately. Some feelings are combinations of two or more of the four categories.

The following list may help you to develop a vocabulary of emotions as you learn to express your feelings in a direct, open, honest manner.

MAD	SAD	GLAD	SCARED	COMBINATION
irritated	unhappy	pleased	anxious	guilty
annoyed	disappointed	happy	worried	jealous
angry	despondent	joyful	fearful	frustrated
ticked off	blue	delighted	concerned	embarrassed
furious	hurt	effervescent	afraid	uncomfortable
miffed	grieved	comfortable	nervous	confused
upset	down	up	inhibited	perplexed
outraged	lonely	excited	uncertain	torn

You can add to the list. Because each person chooses and experiences feelings in a unique way, some feeling words will fit into different categories. Some people use 'upset' to mean 'MAD' while others use it to mean 'SAD'. You decide the words which best reflect your feelings.

Developing emotional awareness

For the next week or two, when you feel an emotion, stop and ask 'What am I feeling – mad, sad or scared?' When you identify your feeling, make yourself aware of the underlying self-talk associated with it. Learn to recognise the physical symptoms related to that feeling. What signals accompany anger, fear, sadness and joy? Recognising these physical clues will help you to increase your emotional awareness. This is the first step towards expressing your feelings assertively.

In the next section on behaviour you will learn more about word choices to express not only your feelings, but also your opinions, thoughts, facts etc. Other guidelines for assertive behaviour will also be provided which will reinforce your assertive words.

CHAPTER 4
Changing Your Behaviour

Now that you have an understanding about how to change your THINKING and FEELING patterns, you need some information about changing BEHAVIOUR. This will help you to learn about the significance of word choices and the other behaviour styles that accompany your words. As you work through this chapter keep yourself aware of how new THINKING and FEELING support your new BEHAVIOUR choices. Using assertive words and behaviour is very difficult without an assertive philosophy. Assertive words and actions may not ring true if your thoughts and feelings are not in concert.

Choose assertive words carefully

To communicate thoughts, feelings, and opinions assertively, you need to choose words that are direct, honest, appropriate and respectful. Some words simply do not fit these criteria and therefore cannot be delivered assertively. Words are only one aspect of being assertive, but you must have assertive words if you are to be assertive with others.

Basic guidelines for assertive word choice:

- Use 'I-statements' rather than 'you statements'.
  Compare the following:
  'You always interrupt my stories!' (Aggressive)
  'I would like to tell my stories without interruption.' (Assertive)

'You embarrassed me in front of all those people.' (Aggressive)
'I felt embarrassed when you said that in front of all those people.' (Assertive)

- Use factual descriptions instead of judgements or exaggerations.
  Compare the following:
  'This is sloppy work.' (Aggressive)
  'The punctuation in your report needs work. Also, your headings are spaced inconsistently.' (Assertive)

  'If you don't change your attitude, you're going to be in real trouble.' (Aggressive)
  'If you continue to arrive after 8.00 am I will be required to place you on two days' probation without pay.' (Assertive)

- Express thoughts, feelings, and opinions reflecting ownership.
  Compare the following:
  'He makes me angry!' (Denies ownership of feelings)
  'I get angry when he breaks his promises!' (Assertive and owns feelings)

  'The only sensible policy is to match the competition.' (States *opinion* as fact; Aggressive, controlling)
  'I believe matching the competition is the best policy.' (Owns opinion; Assertive)

  'Don't you think we should postpone this for now?' (Passive, indirect, denies ownership)
  'I think postponing this question would allow us time to gather more data.' (Owns thought)

- Use clear, direct requests or directives (commands) when you want others to do something rather than hinting, being indirect, or presuming.
  Compare the following:
  'Would you mind taking this to John?' (Indirect, only

enquires about willingness)
'Will you please take this to John?' (Assertive request)
'Please take this to John.' (Assertive directive)

'Why don't you stop on the way home and pick up some milk?' (Indirect, asks the other to think about not doing it)
'Will you please pick up some milk on your way home?' (Assertive request)
'Please pick up some milk on your way home.' (Assertive directive)

'I need five copies of this for my meeting.' (Presumes the other will make copies when need is verbalised, does not direct or ask for anything)
'Will you please make five copies of this for my meeting?' (Assertive request)
'Please make five copies of this for my meeting.' (Assertive directive)

People avoid being direct and honest because they learned to think it was impolite or pushy. Unfortunately, while attempting to avoid being inappropriate we sometimes choose words that communicate a lack of respect. Sometimes we are so 'careful' we don't communicate the real message.

When we say 'don't you think?' instead of 'I think', we are communicating indirectly. If you really listen to the words they sound condescending. When you ask 'why don't you?' instead of 'will you?', you are literally asking a person to find reasons not to. When you say 'I need' and presume someone will take care of your needs, you communicate a lack of respect or an air of superiority. If you say 'I need' or 'I want', learn to add a request or directive in order to be assertive.

These may seem like picky details. You might say, 'Most people know what is meant when I use those words, so what's the difference?' The difference is that you may be getting expected results only because people are able to figure out your unexpressed intentions. You may not be getting their respect. Continuing to use improper words will reinforce old habits and interfere with your being truly assertive. You can increase your success rate and improve relationships by using the direct, honest, assertive words.

Some dos and don'ts

The following are some DOS and DON'TS for assertive word selection.

	DO		DON'T
	Say 'No' politely and firmly		Say 'I can't' or 'I won't be able to'.
	Express feelings honestly: 'I'm angry', 'I'm disappointed', 'I'm delighted', 'I enjoy being with you'.		Depersonalise feelings or deny ownership: 'You make me mad', 'That's disappointing'. 'That's delightful', 'You make me feel so good'.
	Be realistic, respectful and honest:		Exaggerate, minimise, or use sarcasm:
say	'This is the third month in a row your report has been late.'	say	'You are never on time with your reports.'
say	'Thank you for asking. I prefer no smoking in my car.'	say	'We wouldn't want to strain your will power!'
	Express preferences and priorities:		Don't defer to be sociable or agree unwillingly:
say	'I don't have a particular film to suggest. I do want to avoid violent ones.		'I don't care – whatever everyone else wants is all right with me.'

Time to practise

With the above guidelines fresh in mind, write some assertive words on a sheet of paper that are appropriate for the following situations:

1. You did not understand what someone just told you and want them to restate their message.

2. You believe you deserve a rise and decide to ask your boss directly.
3. You have been invited to a social event that does not interest you. Decline the invitation.
4. You are pleased about what someone has done. Tell them your feelings.

After you have completed this exercise, have someone you respect provide feedback about what you wrote. Ideally, this person will have knowledge of the behaviour styles and criteria and will be able to help you to improve word choices.

A quick self-check question is: 'WHAT DO THESE WORDS INVITE FROM THE OTHER?' If the words invite cooperation, respect, and feeling, ALL RIGHT, they are assertive. If the words invite defensiveness, retaliation, or feeling, UNACCEPTABLE, they are aggressive. If the words invite disregard, disrespect, pity or feeling superior to you, they are non-assertive.

Body language

We have now seen that your word choice is critically important. Perhaps even more essential is HOW YOU SAY THEM. Your delivery of the message makes all the difference. Most people use the phrase 'body language' to refer to all aspects of interpersonal communication beyond the choice of words. Everything becomes important when a message is being delivered: voice tone, volume, inflection, pace; eye contact or lack of it; facial expression; gestures, movements, or lack thereof; posture; muscle tension; changes in skin colouring; clothing, hair style etc.

Staying aware of all aspects of body language continuously is not possible. Having some awareness is very important in your assertiveness training. Even though the other person might not be able to list all your body language signals during an interaction, they respond and interpret them unconsciously as part of 'decoding' your 'encoded' message. This process is automatic, constant, and complex.

Don't be discouraged. You don't have to monitor constantly all aspects of body language to be assertive. You do, however, need to learn some body language signals to accompany your words that will help you to be perceived as an assertive person. Perfection is not required for success.

On the next page are some basic body language signals which have been categorised according to how most people perceive them. As you read the list, you may want to act out each one to get a better sense of what the signal communicates.

Body language signals

	Non-assertive	Assertive	Aggressive
POSTURE	slumped shoulders forward shifting often chin down sitting: legs entwined	erect but relaxed shoulders straight few shifts, comfortable head straight or slight tilt sitting: legs together or crossed	erect, tense, rigid shoulders back jerky shifts or firm in place chin up or thrust forward sitting: heels on desk, hands behind head or tensely leaning forward
GESTURES	fluttering hands twisting motions shoulder shrugs frequent head nodding	casual hand movements relaxed hands hands open, palms out occasional head nodding	chopping or jabbing with hands clenched hands or pointing sweeping arms sharp, quick nods
FACIAL EXPRESSION	lifted eyebrows, pleading look, wide-eyed, rapid blinking nervous or guilty smile chewing lower lip shows anger with averted eyes, blushing, guilty look	relaxed, thoughtful, caring or concerned look, few blinks genuine smile relaxed mouth shows anger with flashing eyes, serious look, slight flush of colour	furrowed brow, tight jaw tense look, unblinking glare patronising or sarcastic smile tight lips shows anger with disapproving scowl, very firm mouth or bared teeth, extreme flush
VOICE	quiet, soft, higher pitch ers, ahs, hesitations stopping in 'midstream' nervous laughter statements sound like questions with voice tone rising at the end	resonant, firm, pleasant smooth, even-flowing comfortable delivery laughter only with humour voice tones stay even when making statement	steely quiet or loud, harsh 'biting off' words, precise measured delivery sarcastic laughter statements sound like orders or pronouncements

Non-assertive, assertive or aggressive?

Given the list of body language signals on the previous page, how would you classify the following? (NAS = Non-assertive, AS = Assertive, AG = Aggressive)

______ 1. Elbows out, fist on hips

______ 2. Touching someone's forearm as you speak to them

______ 3. While walking, putting an arm around someone's shoulders and firmly grasping their shoulder on side opposite you

______ 4. Shifting repeatedly from one foot to the other while standing

______ 5. Constantly nodding head up and down

______ 6. Leaning back, propping feet on desk, grasping hands behind head

______ 7. Looking at toes while speaking

______ 8. Leaning forward with hands grasped, elbows on knees while seated, facing someone

______ 9. Rapidly tapping pencil (like a drumstick) while listening

______ 10. Sitting with elbows on table, hands together, chin on hands while listening

______ 11. Standing with arms folded while listening

______ 12. Standing with arms folded, head tilted, and legs crossed

______ 13. Looking over the tops of eyeglasses

______ 14. Twirling a pencil with fingers at each end while talking

______ 15. Elbows on table, hands together at fingertips forming a 'steeple'

Now check your answers below.

Check your answers

The following answers represent the most common interpretation of the above signals. Part of the difficulty with developing body language awareness and skills is that such 'signals' can be interpreted differently by different people.

1. Aggressive. This posture makes a person look larger, much like birds fluff out their feathers, mammals raise neck hairs, and some fish and reptiles inflate themselves.
2. Assertive. This may be a comforting gesture or a way to communicate emphasis.
3. Aggressive. This entraps the other person and is a controlling manoeuvre rather than an affectionate or comforting one.
4. Non-assertive. The shifting movement communicates anxiety.
5. Non-assertive. Head bobbing usually signals 'I want to please you'. Occasional nods may communicate attentiveness.
6. Aggressive. Most people perceive this as a power display.
7. Non-assertive. Looking down frequently or steadily communicates anxiety.
8. Assertive. This probably will signal interest and attentiveness.
9. Aggressive. When the tapping communicates impatience or boredom, it might come across as nervousness (accompanying signals make the difference).
10. Assertive. This looks relaxed and attentive.
11. Aggressive. This is the most frequent interpretation. Others include 'closed mind', impatient, bored, uncaring, and defensive.
12. Non-assertive. This posture usually signals deference and it is almost impossible to stay still. It could appear relaxed with a peer.
13. Aggressive. This signal usually looks disapproving or threatening.
14. Non-assertive. Twirling the pencil probably communicates anxiety. Doing it while listening to someone could signal impatience.
15. Aggressive. This is another subtle power display.

It is important to understand that body language signals have many possible interpretations. A single body language cue is often not enough for an accurate 'reading' of the communication. Body language signals must be interpreted in total. Like a detective, it is necessary to discover and interpret a number of clues to solve the 'body language mystery'.

One way to become more sensitive to body language is to become a 'people watcher with a purpose'. This can help you to develop a better awareness of how body language communicates non-assertive, assertive, and aggressive behaviour. You will notice that people not only use different words with each style, but also communicate these styles with their body language signals. Recognising non-assertive and aggressive signals can help you learn to avoid using them when your goal is to be perceived as assertive.

One way to develop your assertiveness is to find an assertive person and observe this person's behaviour. Take note of the words and body language the person uses. Most of what we learned as children was through observation. The system still works. Following a good role model is an easy and fun way to learn how to become more assertive.

Body language makes a difference! Jurors are often influenced by the body language of the opposing counsels and witnesses. In a personal injury case, the counsel representing the plaintiff strutted, smirked, and used a loud, nasal voice while questioning witnesses. When the defence counsel would comment or ask questions, the plaintiff's counsel would make disbelieving or disapproving facial expressions.

The defence counsel was not a strong personality. He spoke in a quiet voice. He slumped when he sat and walked with poor posture. His movements were jerky and uncertain.

The jury seemed offended by the behaviour of the plaintiff's counsel. On the other hand, they were not impressed with the defendant's counsel. Without knowing any of the evidence in the case, can you predict which counsel won?

Obviously, the evidence and testimony were factors; however, the consistently obnoxious behaviour of the plaintiff's counsel was the key factor. The jurors were so 'turned off' by his aggressiveness towards the witnesses that they decided for the defence. A respectful, assertive counsel could have won for the plaintiff.

Stop signs

There are several signals that will indicate when you are heading down the wrong road. These signals can be either non-assertive or aggressive. Read and learn the signals. Practise using what you learn. It's all right to stop and say something like 'Excuse me. Let me start over again.' Others will respect your efforts to be assertive.

Saying 'you should', 'you must', 'you have to'. Restate as either a request or a directive.

Using exaggerated words – 'obviously', 'absolutely', 'always', 'never', 'impossible'.

Restate with more realistic and factual words.

Saying 'you know', 'maybe', 'rather', 'only', 'just'. Restate in a more direct, confident manner without the 'wishy-washy' qualifiers.

Asking 'can you?', 'could you?', 'would you?', 'why don't you?', 'would you mind?', 'do you think you might?'. Request by asking 'will you please?' – it is the only question that truly asks for action and a commitment!

Using 'it', 'that', 'one', 'you', 'we', instead of 'I'. State your thoughts with 'I think', your opinions with 'I believe', and your feelings with 'I feel (mad, sad, glad, scared)' or 'I am (mad, sad, glad, scared)'.

Green lights

The following signals indicate that you are on the right road and communicating assertively. Keep going when you have green lights!

GO

When you feel relaxed, comfortable, and stress free. These are positive signs that you are being assertive.

GO

When the person with whom you are interacting displays attentiveness, comfort, cooperation, and respect. When you see no signals of bad feelings, rebellion, disregard or defensiveness, you are being assertive.

GO

When another says 'all right', 'certainly', or 'I'll be glad to' in response to your request or directive. When others do what you wanted with no indication of resentment or discomfort, you have good evidence you were assertive.

GO

When others are assertive with you. When they communicate their honest thoughts, feelings, opinions, wants and needs in a direct and respectful manner, they are affirming your assertive behaviour with them.

CHAPTER 5
Expanding Your Assertiveness

Now that you understand the basic philosophy of being assertive and have some practice with the words and body language that communicate assertiveness, you can begin to expand the range of your assertive abilities and skills.

Within the assertive behaviour style, there are different ways to be assertive. Four distinct styles are discussed in this chapter. Everyone has a natural assertive style which comes from his or her basic personality. You will probably recognise yours as you read the following descriptions. Which is your assertive style?

Four assertive styles

1. Supporting/Caring

This style communicates warmth, nurturing, and concern for others. Content is presented in a direct, honest and respectful manner. It maintains an awareness for the feelings of others. Those who naturally use this assertive style are often FEELERS.

2. Directing/Guiding

This is an impersonal style that communicates a no-nonsense, authoritative approach and a concern for results. It is a firm but respectful style using directives rather than requests. It does not come across as being bossy or dictatorial. The directing/guiding style communicates beliefs and opinions appropriately as well as commands. Those who use this style most frequently are DOERS and/or THINKERS.

3. Analytical

This style is also impersonal and matter-of-fact. It communicates facts, information, thoughts, and probabilities. This style uses requests to obtain results rather than directives. Directing/Guiding is a 'tell 'em' style while analytical is an 'ask 'em' style. Analytical is calm and emotionless. It is used most naturally by those in the THINKER group.

4. Expressive

This style is animated, energetic, spontaneous, and emotional. Feelings, likes and dislikes, wants and needs are communicated in this style in an open and expressive manner. Those using this style are usually intuitive, creative, spontaneous and lively. They are normally DOERS or FEELERS.

Did you recognise your natural assertive style? Did you recognise others you know as you read each description? All four styles are assertive because each communicates in an appropriate, direct and honest manner. Everyone uses all styles to some extent, but as individuals, each of us has one as a primary, natural assertive style.

Which style is which? – a quiz

Using the abbreviations listed below, identify which assertive style is used in the following examples. Reading them aloud may help you recognise the differences.

S/C = Supporting/Caring D/G = Directing/Guiding A = Analytical E = Expressive

______ 1. 'The quarterly report indicates a 7 per cent increase in productivity.'

______ 2. 'That's terrific!'

______ 3. 'I really appreciate your summarising all that data for us.'

______ 4. 'It's important to nail down just how that was accomplished.'

______ 5. 'Give me some more details on that new product line.'

______ 6. 'I know you're excited about our new products, Pat, and I would like to hear more about them after we finish the productivity discussion.'

______ 7. 'Thank you Terry. I estimate about 20 minutes will be required to complete the productivity analysis. The next item on the agenda will be new products.'

______ 8. 'Right, let's do it. This productivity stuff is boring and I'd like to get on to a new topic, too!'

______ 9. 'You certainly do like the new ideas, don't you, Chris? Thank you for being patient long enough for us to finish.'

______ 10. 'My analysis revealed three factors which contributed to the productivity improvement. The first was . . . '

Check your answers below.

Answers

1. Analytical. A straightforward statement of facts.
2. Expressive. Spontaneous enthusiasm.
3. Supporting/Caring. A personal acknowledgement with gratitude.
4. Directing/Guiding. A statement of opinion and a concern for results.
5. Directing/Guiding. Commanding someone to provide information.
6. Supporting/Caring. Recognising another's interest and indicating support while preventing a diversion.
7. Analytical. Providing information about timing and upcoming agenda item.
8. Expressive. Action words, stating a dislike and enthusiasm for the suggested new topic.
9. Supporting/Caring. Acknowledging Chris's enthusiasm and expressing appreciation for co-operation.
10. Analytical. Informative, factual, unemotional.

A case history

A Directing/Guiding manager, Joyce had an administrative assistant, Sue, who was a Supporting/Caring person. Sue wanted to help Joyce and was dedicated to doing everything possible to maintain a satisfying relationship. Joyce was unconcerned about the quality of the relationship and concentrated more on getting things done.

Over time, Joyce's continued use of directives began to create stress for Sue. Like most Supporting/Caring people, Sue interpreted commands as uncaring and occasionally heard them as reprimands. Sue's interest in Joyce's family and home life seemed unprofessional to Joyce and was a source of discomfort.

After months of working together, Sue resigned. In the exit interview conducted by the director of personnel, Sue explained that her manager seemed to disapprove of her many efforts to help. Sue said she was leaving to find a job with a boss who would appreciate qualities such as loyalty, devotion and anticipation of needs.

When the director of personnel reviewed the interview with Joyce, the result was amazed perplexity. Joyce explained how her assistant always wanted to talk about families and seemed to hover about, expressing concern about not being able to help more. 'I don't like someone fussing over me all the time. I want my employees to do what I tell them and concentrate on doing their work.'

It is obvious to an informed observer how the manager and assistant failed to understand each other's priorities and style. When those involved don't know about differences in personality styles, they often fail to communicate and will experience stressful relationships.

By learning to recognise and use all four assertive styles, you will be able to communicate more effectively with almost everyone. Once you recognise a style and sensitively match it (at least part of the time) you will improve your communication with that person – even if it was previously difficult to make a connection. An easy way to remember the importance of matching styles is to think of speaking to someone by short wave radio. If you send your message on one channel and they receive on another channel, you will not be able to communicate. When you are both on the same channel, then you can communicate.

Sending assertive messages

The following exercise will allow you to practise sending messages in different styles. Write your responses and then compare your basic usage with the sample provided. IMPORTANT – Do not look at the samples before writing your message. The purpose of this exercise is to practise using what you have learned. If you need help, look at the examples at the beginning of the chapter. Your words do not have to be the same – but the meaning should be similar.

MESSAGE 1: Tell or ask Pat to assist you with a project.

1. Supporting/Caring Style:

2. Directing/Guiding Style:

3. Analytical Style:

4. Expressive Style:

MESSAGE 2: Give Chris feedback about how well she has organised a meeting.

1. Supporting/Caring Style:

2. Directing/Guiding Style:

3. Analytical Style:

4. Expressive Style:

(See sample responses on the next page.)

Compare your responses

Compare your messages with the following examples. Yours may not be exactly like the samples but they should help you to judge how successfully you were able to 'switch channels'. Remember, it is not simply the choice of words that creates a style. Read your messages aloud with appropriate delivery to help you communicate in the different styles.

MESSAGE 1

Supporting/Caring: 'Pat, if you can spare the time, will you please give me some help on this project? Thank you so much.'

Directing/Guiding: 'Pat, please complete this part for me so I can wrap up this project.'

Analytical: 'Pat, if you assist me, I can complete this project this week. Will you organise this section?'

Expressive: 'Pat! Help! I'm swamped—how about running some figures for me?'

MESSAGE 2

Supporting/Caring: 'Chris, I really appreciate how well you organised the conference. Everyone seemed comfortable with the arrangements.'

Directing/Guiding: 'Chris, that was a fine job on the meeting arrangements.'

Analytical: 'Chris, your arrangements for the conference were very complete. The sessions were on time, everyone had all the necessary information, and the meeting ran efficiently.'

Expressive: 'Super job, Chris! Excellent meeting!'

Can you identify these people?

Two business people were seated in the same row in a plane. The middle seat was initially empty. It was a full flight and a third person finally occupied the seat between the two travellers. The person in the middle was a man who also appeared to be travelling for business.

The person by the window asked the man in the middle, 'What is your destination?' The man answered, 'Sharjak.' After a short while the passenger by the window asked, 'What business are you in?' The reply, 'Electronics'. The person by the window made no further attempts to communicate.

The person sitting in the aisle seat had heard the above interaction. This passenger also noticed the middle passenger's expensive suit, costly wristwatch, and eelskin briefcase. Assessing the visual clues and lack of responsiveness to the other person's questions, the aisle passenger said to the man in the middle seat, 'Tell me about what you do.' The man launched into a lengthy explanation of his business, the purpose of the trip, and his past success!

1. Which communication style was used by the window seat passenger?
2. Which style was used by the aisle seat passenger?
3. What was the middle passenger's personality type? (Thinker, Feeler or Doer)

Answers

1. Analytical
2. Directing/Guiding
3. Doer

When the aisle passenger correctly assessed the middle seat passenger as a Doer who did not respond to the Analytical style, this provided information about which style would be successful. Many Doers use a Directing/Guiding style and exhibit pride in what they have achieved with visible signs of success. Using a directive aimed at 'doing' established rapport instantly. The Analytical communicator had no success involving the middle seat passenger in conversation because an inaccurate choice of words was used.

How delivery affects different styles

How you say words when using each style is so important that some suggestions for successful delivery follow:

Supporting/Caring. Use a warm, nurturing, mellow tone of voice. Communicate personal interest, appreciation, concern, gratitude, or empathy, by making good eye contact and using comforting facial expressions (think of a loving grandparent).

Directing/Guiding. Be firm and authoritative, but not harsh or dictatorial. Your delivery should be matter of fact, direct, and serious. Facial involvement is an expression of concentration or purpose.

Analytical. Use an even, no-nonsense, pragmatic delivery. Your facial expression looks alert and thoughtful. You can be polite, but don't show emotion.

Expressive. Everything is expressive! Your voice range and facial expressions are almost limitless. Be animated with your face, hands, and body movements. Show emotion.

Role models can help you learn to use all four assertive styles. As mentioned earlier, it is fun to follow the example of someone whose natural style is one of the four assertive styles. Very likely you have mentally identified someone with a similar style to each of the types described. If not, you should be able to find one of each by listening and observing. It is also possible to find examples of the four assertive styles in television programmes or films. Once you find a role model of the style you want to practise, study that person and adopt those characteristics that seem most effective.

Stay on the right road–goal setting

To avoid taking wrong turns and slipping into former patterns of non-assertive and/or aggressive behaviour, practise assertive behaviour regularly. First take short trips and then longer journeys.

SHORT TRIPS (short-term goals):

1. Once a day during the next week spend 10–15 minutes at the end of each working day writing assertive statements about situations involving you, or observed by you. Use non-assertive and aggressive incidents and write how they could have been handled assertively.
2. Each evening before turning out the light read the 'psychological reprogramming' cards you completed on pages 29–32, after achieving a state of relaxation. Do this for three weeks.
3. At least once each week for the next three weeks initiate a conversation with someone whose natural assertive style is different from your own. Practise using their style. Notice the positive features of their style and try using them yourself.

Short-term goals

By now you probably have some goals you want to accomplish. Write your short-term goals in the spaces below. Remember to make them achievable and positive.

During the next three weeks I WILL:

1.

2.

3.

LONGER JOURNEYS (long-term goals):

1. Enrol and participate in an assertiveness training course or seminar.
2. Identify a situation or activity which you have not handled assertively in the past and plan how to handle it assertively

in the future. Write out what you will say. Practise delivering it with a friend and then do it!

3. Make additional 'reprogramming' cards and use them. Review your old cards on a regular basis.
4. Read books about assertiveness, personal growth or communication skills within the next month. Cassette tape programmes may also be helpful.

Long-term goals

Write the long-term goals you want to achieve.

During the next three months I WILL:

1.

2.

3.

Some of the goals you may want to accomplish might require more than three months. If so, write those goals in the spaces below.

Within the next year I WILL:

1.

2.

3.

Giving yourself credit for success

Reliving a special trip through snapshots or video film can be fun and rekindle feelings of pleasure you experienced originally. In a similar fashion, the following are some suggestions to help you reinforce the success of your new assertiveness skills.

1. Tell a friend or family about a successful assertive experience you had. Ask this person to comment on your success.

2. Keep a journal. Write down your assertive success. The entry does not have to be anything unusual, difficult, or dramatic — just so long as it is assertive behaviour. Review your journal regularly. Reading about past successes can provide a real 'shot' of positive energy whenever you are feeling low.
3. Immediately after you have been assertive and are pleased with the outcome, take a few minutes to mentally 'record' the experience. Close your eyes and *SEE* the scene as vividly as possible– *FEEL* your power, confidence, and satisfaction and *HEAR* your words and voice. While re-experiencing the success with your senses, touch yourself in a predetermined spot (squeeze a thumbnail, pull an earlobe etc) to 'set' the experience. In the future, whenever you want to recall the scene and return to assertiveness, touch yourself in the 'reminder' spot.
4. Re-read this book next week and then again in three months. Re-do the exercises. Compare the results with your earlier work. Define some new short- and long-term goals. The assertive road to interpersonal effectiveness never ends.
5. Share with others. Tell them what you learned about yourself (use I-language!)'. Share your goals. This will increase your commitment to them. Give copies of this book to others and compare notes with them after they have completed it.

CHAPTER 6
Summary and Review

Here is a quick review of what has been presented in this book. There are three fundamental behaviour patterns, non-assertive, assertive and aggressive. Of those styles, assertive behaviour is the most desirable.

First you took a reading of your own assertiveness. Next you learned to identify each behaviour style and you learned about the basic personality groups of Thinkers, Feelers, and Doers. These initial insights were provided to help you move towards a 'win-win' philosophy of assertiveness.

The five Ps of successful change were then presented (protection, potency, permission, practice and proof). Please re-read that section to make sure you do what is required to assure your successful development of assertiveness. Remember that self-fulfilling prophecy is a real phenomenon and follow an assertive philosophy. If you expect to be assertive, you will create more success in your life and influence others in a positive way.

You next learned about the power of psychological reprogramming and were given a way to use it as a tool. You also learned that being assertive requires using direct, honest, respectful words and accompanying body language.

A refinement of your communication skills was then covered which encouraged the development of your abilities to use all four assertive styles. These styles are Supporting/Caring, Directing/Guiding, Analytical, and Expressive, and you had an opportunity to define some short- and long-term goals, and practise creating assertive responses for situations. Finally, you were encouraged to continue along the assertive road to interpersonal effectiveness. This book has given you the tools to help you become assertive–it is up to you to apply what you have learned.